Contents

SCHOLASTIC

GRADE
1

100 Math Practice Pages

New York • Toronto • London • Auckland • Sydney
Mexico City • New Delhi • Hong Kong • Buenos Aires

Teaching *Resources*

Text Credits: Practice Pages 3, 6, 7, 15, 18, 21, 25, 34, 39, 41, and 44 taken and/or adapted from *Solve-the-Riddle Math Practice* by Liane B. Onish © 2009 by Liane B. Onish; Practice Pages 11, 16, 20, 38, 40, 43, and 46 taken and/or adapted from *Practice, Practice, Practice! Addition & Subtraction* by Betsy Franco © 2005 by Betsy Franco; Practice Pages 2, 5, 19, 29, 77, 78, and 99 taken and/or adapted from *Tic-Tac-Math: Grades K–2* by Sue Hanson © 2005 by Sue Hanson. Other Practice Pages from this workbook were previously published in: *Brain-Boosting Math Activities, Grade 1*; *Math Picture Puzzles for Little Learners*; *Math Problem of the Day Practice Mats*; and *Morning Jumpstarts: Math, Grade 1*.

Edited by Mela Ottaiano
Cover design by Lindsey Dekker
Interior design by Melinda Belter

ISBN: 978-0-545-79937-9
Compilation copyright © 2015 by Scholastic Inc.
Illustrations copyright © by Scholastic Inc.
All rights reserved.
Published by Scholastic Inc.
Printed in the U.S.A.

2 3 4 5 6 7 8 9 10   40   22 21 20 19 18 17 16

Introduction

In today's busy classrooms, it is vital to maximize learning time. That's where *100 Math Practice Pages, Grade 1* comes in. The activities in this book are designed to review and reinforce a range of math skills and concepts students will build throughout the year. Each page provides focused individual practice on an essential grade-level skill students are expected to master, including numbers and counting, place value, addition, subtraction, time, measurement, shapes, and graphs.

Reviewing skills students have already learned is a good way to keep their math skills sharp and to point out where revisiting a skill may be beneficial. You know your students best, so feel free to pick and choose among the activities and incorporate them as you see fit. The goal is to build automaticity, fluency, and accuracy.

How to Use This Book

Preview each activity page to ensure that students have the skills needed to complete it. If necessary, walk through its features with your class to provide an overview before you assign it and to make sure students understand the directions. Work out a model problem or two as a class.

The 100 practice pages can be used to enhance the curriculum during math time, to keep fast finishers on task anytime, or as homework.

You'll find an answer key beginning on page 107. If time allows, you might want to review answers with the whole class. This approach provides opportunities for discussion, comparison, extension, reinforcement, and correlation to other skills and lessons. Your observations can direct the kinds of review or reinforcement you may want to add to your lessons. Alternatively, you may find that having students discuss activity solutions and strategies in small groups is another effective way to deepen understanding.

> The engaging activity pages are a great way to help students:
>
> ✓ reinforce key academic skills and concepts
>
> ✓ meet curriculum standards
>
> ✓ prepare for standardized tests
>
> ✓ succeed in school
>
> ✓ become lifelong learners!

Meeting the Standards

Completing the exercises will help students meet the College and Career Readiness Standards for Mathematics, which serve as the backbone for the practice pages in this book. These broad standards were developed to establish a framework of clear educational expectations meant to provide students nationwide with a quality education that prepares them for college and careers. The following list details how the activities in this book align with the standards in the key areas of focus for students in grade 1.

Standards for Mathematics

MATHEMATICAL PRACTICE

1. Make sense of problems and persevere in solving them.
2. Reason abstractly and quantitatively.
3. Construct viable arguments and critique the reasoning of others.
4. Model with mathematics.
5. Use appropriate tools strategically.
6. Attend to precision.
7. Look for and make use of structure.
8. Look for and express regularity in repeating reasoning.

MATHEMATICAL CONTENT

✓ Operations and Algebraic Thinking
✓ Number and Operations in Base Ten
✓ Measurement and Data
✓ Geometry

Name _____ Date _____

Ice Dweller

Connect the dots in order.

Start at 1.

What picture did you make?

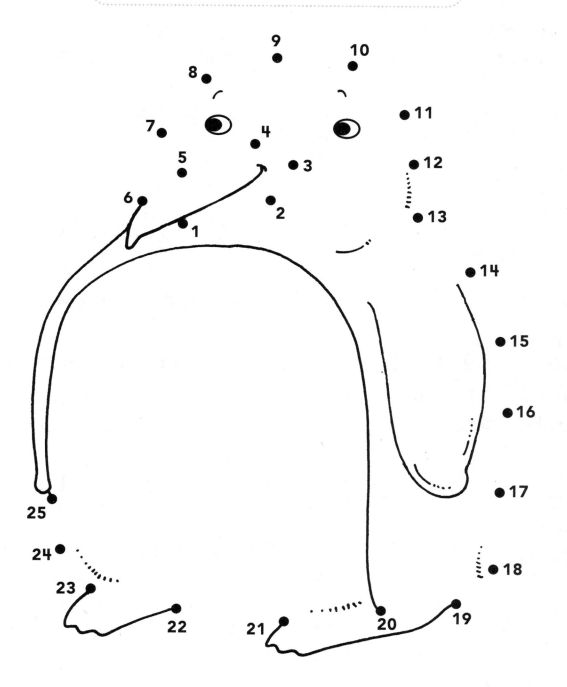

100 Math Practice Pages, Grade 1 © 2015 • Scholastic Teaching Resources

Name _____ Date _____

What's the Number?

Complete each problem.

Fill in the missing numbers.

1 ____ 3 4 ____

6 7 ____ 9 ____

Circle all the number ones that you see.

41   10   100   7

16   17   52   101

31   91   6   24

Write the number that comes after each number below.

2 ____   10 ____

4 ____   16 ____

Circle the larger number.

7 or 17   9 or 4

12 or 2   1 or 5

3 or 7   8 or 0

Name _____ Date _____

Where was the owl
when the lights went out?

Write the missing numbers.
Solve the riddle using your answers.

28, 29, 30, _____, 32
A

27, 28, 29, _____, 31
D

25, 26, 27, _____, 29
E

26, 27, 28, _____, 30
F

31, 32, 33, _____, 35
H

37, 38, 39, _____, 41
I

33, 34, 35, _____, 37
N

35, 36, 37, _____, 39
K

40, 41, 42, _____, 44
T

38, 39, 40, _____, 42
R

39, 40, 41, _____, 43
S

46, 47, 48, _____, 50
W

Solve the Riddle! Write the letter that goes with each number.

____ ____   ____ ____ ____
40   36   43   34   28

____ ____ ____ ____
30   31   41   38

100 Math Practice Pages, Grade 1 © 2015 • Scholastic Teaching Resources

Name _____

Date _____

Finding Fruit

Write how many strawberries.

 🍓🍓	2
 🍓🍓🍓🍓	
 🍓🍓🍓🍓🍓	
 🍓🍓🍓	
 🍓🍓🍓🍓🍓🍓	

Write how many bananas.

🍌🍌🍌	
🍌🍌🍌🍌🍌🍌🍌	
🍌🍌🍌🍌	
🍌🍌🍌🍌🍌🍌🍌🍌🍌🍌	
🍌🍌🍌🍌🍌🍌	

Name _____   Date _____

Know Your Numbers

Complete each problem.

Count to:

- 8 but begin at 2.
- 9 but begin at 3.
- 12 but begin at 5.
- 10 but begin at 4.
- 20 but begin at 11.

Circle the smaller number.

14 or 40   19 or 31

2 or 5   11 or 15

29 or 18   38 or 7

Write the numbers from 11 to 19 in order. Use the spaces below.

____ ____ ____

____ ____ ____

____ ____ ____

Circle all of the number fives you see.

96   15   55

4   5   105

525   65   17

What kinds of stories does a ship captain read to his kids?

Write the missing numbers.
Solve the riddle using your answers.

52, 53, 54, ____, 56 A	56, 57, 58 ____, 60 B
53, 54, 55, ____, 57 C	48, 49, 50, ____, 52 F
50, 51, 52, ____, 54 G	57, 58, 59, ____, 61 E
54, 55, 56, ____, 58 I	66, 67, 68, ____, 70 L
68, 69, 70, ____, 72 R	71, 72, 73, ____, 75 S
65, 66, 67, ____, 69 T	69, 70, 71, ____, 73 Y

Solve the Riddle!   Write the letter that goes with each number.

____   ____   ____   ____   ____
51   60   71   71   72

____   ____   ____   ____   ____
68   55   69   60   74

Name _____ Date _____

Up in the Clouds

Write the missing numbers in each cloud.

73, 74, _____ , 76, 77

79, 80, _____ , 82, 83

82, 83, _____ , 85, 86

77, 78, _____ , 80, 81

85, 86, _____ , 88, 89

89, 90, _____ , 92, 93

94, 95, _____ , 97, 98

96, 97, 98, 99, _____

100 Math Practice Pages, Grade 1 © 2015 • Scholastic Teaching Resources

Name _____ Date _____

Daisy Days

If the number word is for	Color the space
1	Orange
2	Green
3	Yellow
4	Brown
5	Purple

Color Key

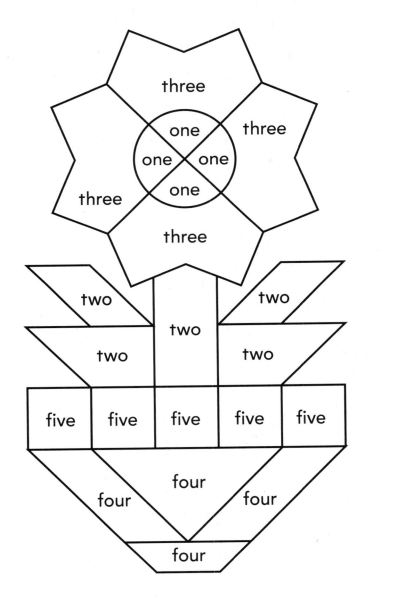

Name _____ Date _____

Ready to Ride

If the number word is for	Color the space
6	Gray
7	Yellow
8	Red
9	Black
10	Brown

Color Key

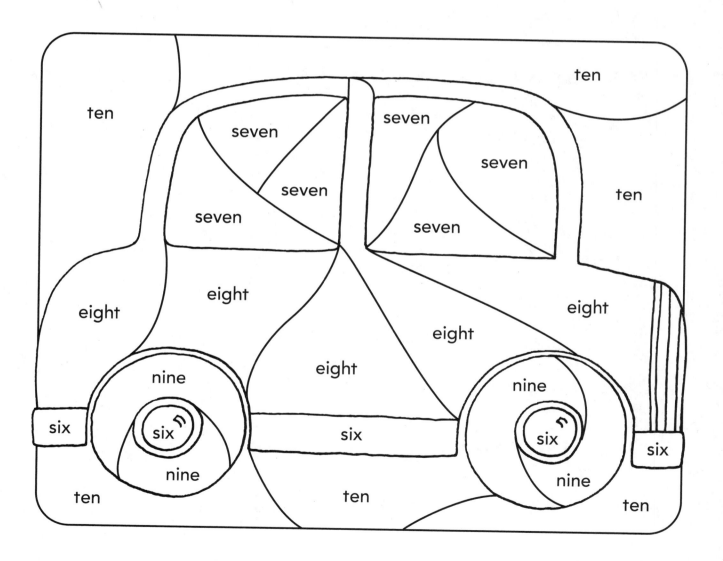

In Order . . .

Follow the directions.

1. Color the **third** ⭐ red.

2. Color the **ninth** ⭐ blue.

3. Color the **sixth** ⭐ green.

4. ✔ the **second** ⭐ .

5. **X** the **eighth** ⭐ .

6. Write **F** on the **fourth** ⭐ .

7. Write **S** on the **seventh** ⭐ .

8. Write **1** on the **first** ⭐ .

9. Write **10** on the **tenth** ⭐ .

10. The _____ ⭐ is empty.

Name _____ Date _____

What's at the Store?

It's time to add up items at the toy store. Read each problem. Then write an equation to answer the question. Use the back of the page to show how you got your answers.

1 7 toy puppies
5 toy kittens

_____ + _____ = _____

How many
toy animals
are in the store? _____

2 9 card games
6 board games

_____ + _____ = _____

How many
games are
in the store? _____

3 7 ring floats
6 flat floats

_____ + _____ = _____

How many
floats are
in the store? _____

4 6 fire trucks
8 dump trucks

_____ + _____ = _____

How many
toy trucks are
in the store? _____

5 9 talking books
8 pop-up books

_____ + _____ = _____

How many
books are
in the store? _____

6 4 baseballs
7 footballs

_____ + _____ = _____

How many
balls are
in the store? _____

100 Math Practice Pages, Grade 1 © 2015 • Scholastic Teaching Resources

Name _____ Date _____

Take Away

Write the subtraction problem.

1.

 _____ − _____ = _____

2.

 _____ − _____ = _____

3.

 _____ − _____ = _____

Name _____ Date _____

Doggie Math

Add or subtract. Use the key.

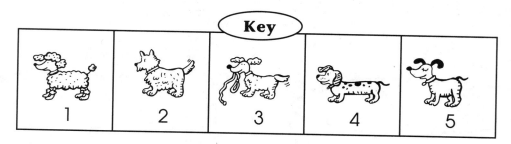

1. _____ + _____ = _____

2. _____ + _____ = _____

3. _____ + _____ = _____

4. _____ − _____ = _____

5. _____ − _____ = _____

6. _____ − _____ = _____

Name _____ Date _____

Decorate Your Birthday Cake

My birthday cake
last year

My birthday cake
this year

My birthday cake
2 years from now

My birthday cake
5 years from now

100 Math Practice Pages, Grade 1 © 2015 • Scholastic Teaching Resources

Name _____

Date _____

What kind of cookies do birds like best?

Add.

Solve the riddle using your answers.

3 + 5 = _____
A

0 + 3 = _____
L

4 + 2 = _____
C

4 + 6 = _____
E

7 + 2 = _____
H

1 + 0 = _____
P

8 + 3 = _____
S

1 + 1 = _____
T

2 + 2 = _____
R

5 + 2 = _____
I

1 + 4 = _____
O

6 + 6 = _____
N

Solve the Riddle!   Write the letter that goes with each number.

___ ___ ___ ___ ___ ___ ___ ___ ___
  6   9   5   6   5   3   8   2   10

___ ___ ___ ___ ___
  6   9   7   4   1

Name _____ Date _____

Box of Chocolates

Cindy Chipmunk had 10 chocolates in each box of candy. She opened the boxes to taste the chocolates inside. Look at how many chocolates are in each box now. Then answer the question. Write an equation to show how you got your answer. The first one has been done for you.

1 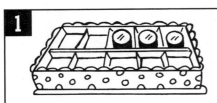 $10 - 3 = 7$ How many chocolates did Cindy eat? ___7___	**2** 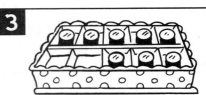 How many chocolates did Cindy eat? _____	**3** 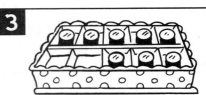 How many chocolates did Cindy eat? _____
4 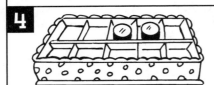 How many chocolates did Cindy eat? _____	**5** 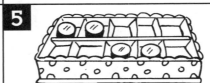 How many chocolates did Cindy eat? _____	**6** 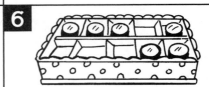 How many chocolates did Cindy eat? _____
7 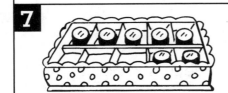 How many chocolates did Cindy eat? _____	**8** 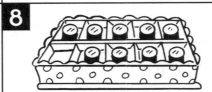 How many chocolates did Cindy eat? _____	**9** 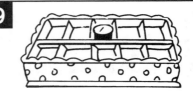 How many chocolates did Cindy eat? _____

100 Math Practice Pages, Grade 1 © 2015 • Scholastic Teaching Resources

Bright Light

Write the answer for each problem.
Connect the dots in the order of your answers.
What picture did you make?

a. $4 - 1 =$ ☐

b. $8 - 2 =$ ☐

c. $12 - 3 =$ ☐

d. $9 - 2 =$ ☐

e. $9 - 5 =$ ☐

f. $10 - 0 =$ ☐

g. $8 - 7 =$ ☐

h. $10 - 2 =$ ☐

i. $12 - 7 =$ ☐

j. $5 - 3 =$ ☐

k. $11 - 1 =$ ☐

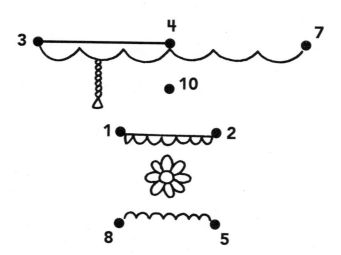

Name _____ Date _____

What does the ocean do when it sees the beach?

Circle the two numbers that make 10. Then add. Solve the riddle using your answers.

Example:

$⑤ + ⑤ + 10 = 20$

$3 + 7 + 4 = $ _____
W

$5 + 1 + 5 = $ _____
R

$6 + 4 + 9 = $ _____
V

$8 + 2 + 10 = $ _____
A

$5 + 3 + 7 = $ _____
I

$3 + 6 + 4 = $ _____
S

$2 + 7 + 8 = $ _____
E

$6 + 2 + 4 = $ _____
N

$5 + 8 + 5 = $ _____
T

Solve the Riddle!   Write the letter that goes with each number.

_____ _____   _____ _____ _____ _____ _____ .
  15   18   14   20   19   17   13

   100 Math Practice Pages, Grade 1 © 2015 • Scholastic Teaching Resources

Name _____ Date _____

Working With Numbers

Complete each problem.

Write the number next to each word.

twenty _____

thirty _____

forty _____

fifty _____

Count backward by 1s. Write the numbers.

20 19 _____ _____

_____ _____ _____

_____ _____ _____

You have 5 crayons. If you give away 2 of your crayons, how many crayons will you have left?

_____ crayons

On the back of this paper, draw these animals in this order:

- The cat is first.

- The fish is second.

- The dog is third.

Name _____   Date _____

Fun With Doubles

Write an equation for each problem. Then find the sum. The first one has been done for you.

1 How many tails?

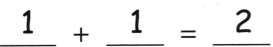

__2__

__1__ + __1__ = __2__

2 How many tennis balls?

____

____ + ____ = ____

3 How many wheels?

____

____ + ____ = ____

4 How many toes?

____

____ + ____ = ____

5 How many spaces?

____

____ + ____ = ____

6 How many spots?

____

____ + ____ = ____

7 How many soccer players?

____

____ + ____ = ____

8 How many eggs?

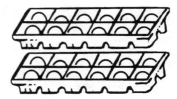

____

____ + ____ = ____

Name _____   Date _____

Why didn't the sad frog jump?

Add or subtract.

Solve the riddle using your answers.

21 – 5 = _____
     A

20 – 9 = _____
     Y

18 + 4 = _____
     H

13 + 6 = _____
     S

24 – 6 = _____
     E

14 – 8 = _____
     W

16 + 7 = _____
     N

17 + 3 = _____
     U

23 + 2 = _____
     O

15 + 9 = _____
     P

19 – 5 = _____
     T

25 – 16 = _____
     R

Solve the Riddle!   Write the letter that goes with each number.

___ ___   ___ ___ ___   ___ ___ ___
22 18   6 16 19   14 25 25

___ ___ ___ ___ ___ ___ ___.
20 23 22 25 24 24 11

Name _____ Date _____

How Many Bees?

Circle sets of ten.

Write the number of tens and ones.

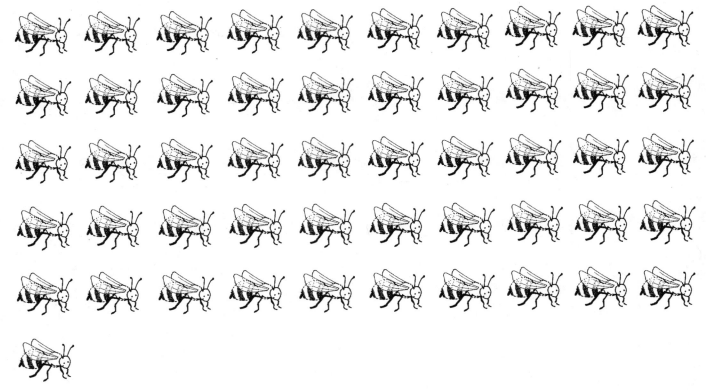

_____ tens _____ ones   What is the number? _____

Quick Review

Match each word to its number.

eleven   fifteen   twelve   thirteen   ten

13   11   10   15   12

Name _____ Date _____

Circle Sets

Complete each problem.
Count. Circle sets of ten.
Write how many.

_____ tens _____ ones

_____ tens _____ ones

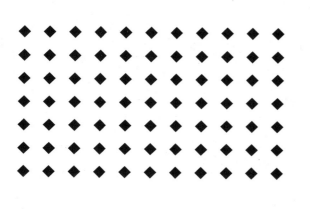

_____ tens _____ ones

_____ tens _____ ones

100 Math Practice Pages, Grade 1 © 2015 • Scholastic Teaching Resources

Name _____ Date _____

Dotty Math

Write how many.

▦▦▦▦▦ · · · ·	
▦▦▦▦▦ · · · · ·	
▦▦▦▦▦ · · · · · ·	
▦▦▦▦▦ · · · · · · ·	
▦▦▦▦▦ · · · · · · · ·	
▦▦▦▦▦ · · · · · · · · ·	

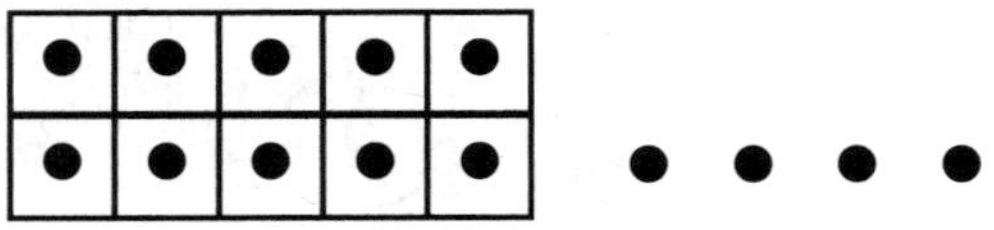

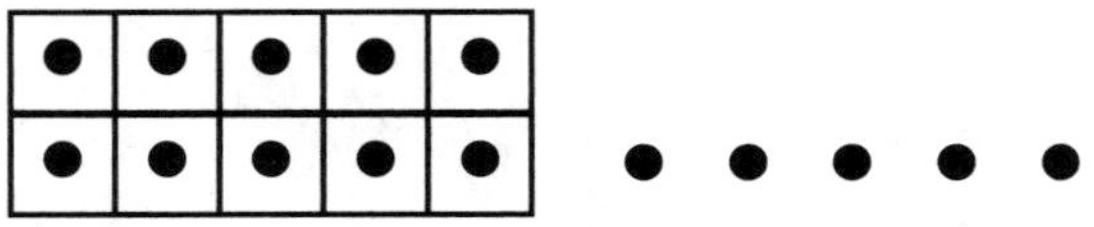

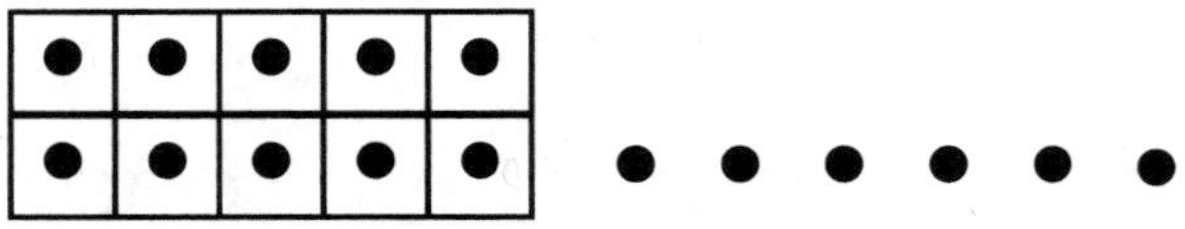

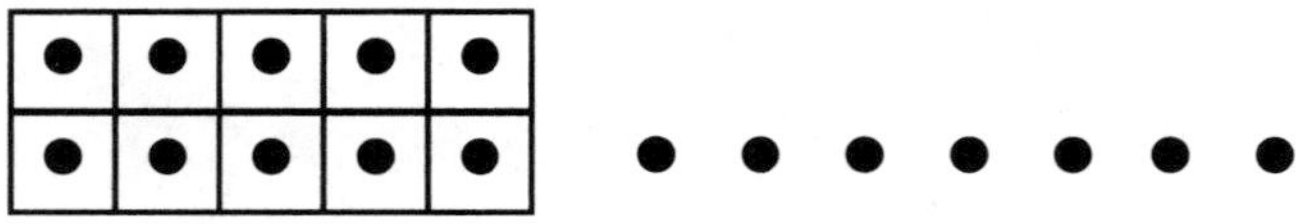

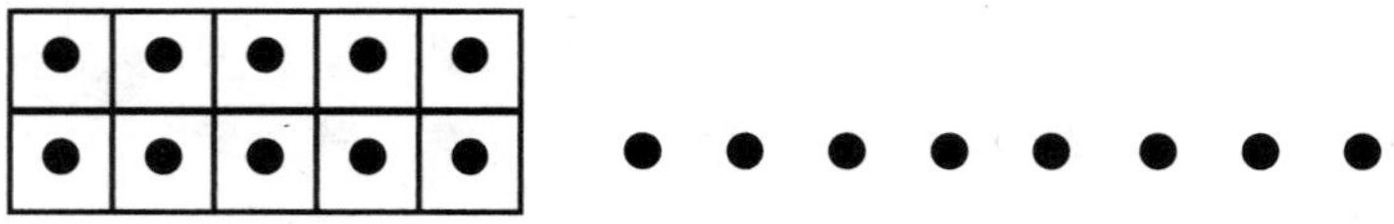

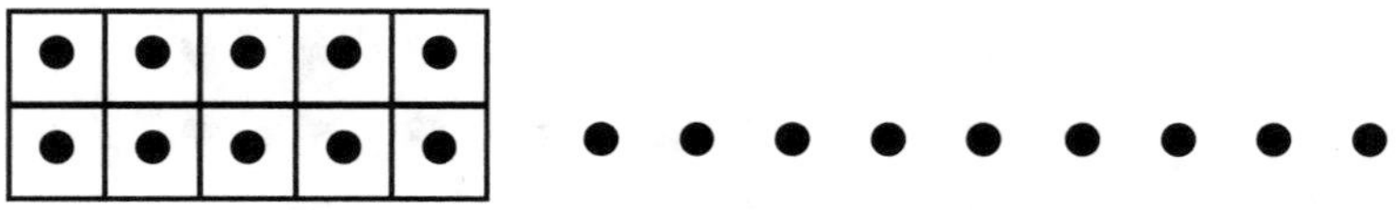

What animals never tell the truth?

Read the words and write the number.
Solve the riddle using your answers.

| two tens and ten ones _____ | five tens and thirteen ones _____ |
| F | I |

| four tens and sixteen ones _____ | five tens and sixteen ones _____ |
| S | M |

| two tens and fifteen ones _____ | two tens and twenty ones _____ |
| E | B |

| one ten and eighteen ones _____ | seven tens and seventeen ones _____ |
| R | A |

| eight tens and eleven ones _____ | six tens and twelve ones _____ |
| N | P |

Solve the Riddle!   Write the letter that goes with each number.

___ ___ - ___ ___ ___ - ___ ___ ___ ___
87 66   30 63 40   63 87 91 56

Name _____   Date _____

Under the Sea

Find the answer to each problem.

If the number	Color the fish
2 is in the ones place	Orange
2 is in the tens place	Yellow
5 is in the ones place	Red
5 is in the tens place	Green

Color Key

100 Math Practice Pages, Grade 1 © 2015 • Scholastic Teaching Resources

Name _____ Date _____

Mystery Question

Decode the mystery question.

Circle each number in the ones place.

Write the letter on the line that goes with each circled number.

M	D	O	Y	R	A	I	N	H	U
80	62	16	91	47	34	59	28	65	73

__ __ W
5 6

__ __ __ __
0 4 8 1

__ __ __ __ S
5 6 3 7

__ __   __   __ __ __ ?
9 8   4   2 4 1

Write the answer: _____

Write the number.

1. _____

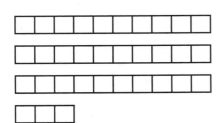

2. _____

100 Math Practice Pages, Grade 1 © 2015 • Scholastic Teaching Resources

Name _____ Date _____

Number Sort

Sort each number. Write it in the chart where
it belongs. Then write your own number that can
go in each area.

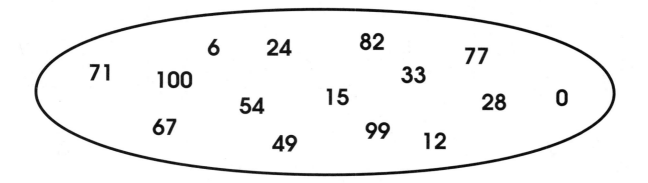

Numbers < 25	Numbers 26 to 70	Numbers > 70

Numbers All Around!

Complete each problem.

Count the dots on each square. Write >, <, or = to compare the numbers.

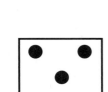

Read each numeral and number word. Write >, <, or = to compare the numbers.

3	six
6	seven
7	two
2	three

Read each numeral and number word. Write >, <, or = to compare the numbers.

ten	2
four	6
five	4
nine	1

Count the dots on each square. Write >, <, or = to compare the numbers.

Name _____ Date _____

Greater Than or Less Than?

Compare the numbers. Use the number line.

Write > or < in each number sentence.

11   12   13   14   15   16   17   18   19   20

1. 11 ____ 18

2. 15 ____ 13

3. 16 ____ 19

4. 17 ____ 16

5. 14 ____ 11

6. 12 ____ 20

Quick Review

1. Color the 3rd grape.

2. Color the 5th grape.

Name _____ Date _____

Busy Bees

Help the bees get to the flowers.
Find the answer to each problem.

If the answer is	Color the space
Less than 10	Orange
From 10 to 20	Yellow
Greater than 20	Red

Color Key

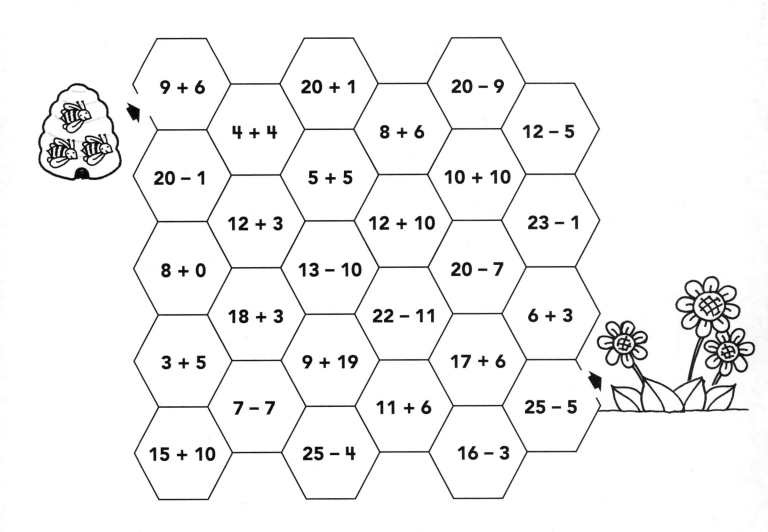

100 Math Practice Pages, Grade 1 © 2015 • Scholastic Teaching Resources

Name _____

Date _____

Follow the Directions

Follow the directions to complete
each problem.

Fill in the
missing numbers.

25, ___, 27, ___, 29, 30

___, 34, ___, 36, 37, 38

58, 59, ___, 61, 62, ___

Circle the eleventh dot.
Draw a square around the
seventeenth dot.

• • • • • • • • • • • • • •

• • • • • • • • • • • • • •

• • • • • • • • • • • • • •

Write > or < in the circle to
compare the numbers.

27 ◯ 37

96 ◯ 95

43 ◯ 34

Add or subtract.

$$\begin{array}{r} 12 \\ +\ 2 \\ \hline \end{array}$$

$$\begin{array}{r} 22 \\ +\ 2 \\ \hline \end{array}$$

$$\begin{array}{r} 17 \\ -\ 5 \\ \hline \end{array}$$

$$\begin{array}{r} 23 \\ -\ 11 \\ \hline \end{array}$$

Name _____ Date _____

Crawly Critter

Connect the dots in order.

Start at 2, then skip-count by 2.

What picture did you make?

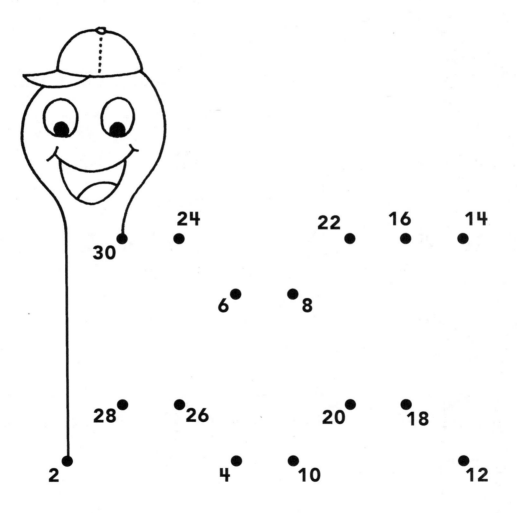

What do little dogs eat at the movies?

Count down by 2. Write the missing numbers.
Solve the riddle using your answers.

40, 38, 36, _____
B

22, 20, 18, _____
O

46, 44, 42, _____
D

38, 36, 34, _____
A

30, 28, 26, _____
P

24, 22, 20, _____
T

50, 48, 46, _____
N

12, 10, 8, _____
E

28, 26, 24, _____
U

26, 24, 22, _____
C

34, 32, 30, _____
R

16, 14, 12, _____
S

Solve the Riddle!   Write the letter that goes with each number.

___ ___ ___ ___ ___ ___ ___ ___
34   22   18   18   6   28   6   40

___ ___ ___ - ___ ___ ___ ___
24   22   24   20   16   28   44

Name _____ Date _____

Hand Warmer

Connect the dots in order.

Start at 5, then skip-count by 5.

What picture did you make?

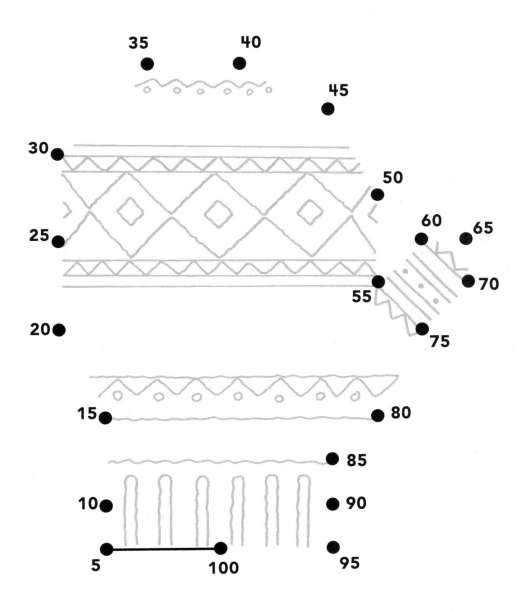

100 Math Practice Pages, Grade 1 © 2015 • Scholastic Teaching Resources

Name _____ Date _____

Soar Into the Sky!

Connect the dots in order.

Start at 10, then skip-count by 10.

What picture did you make?

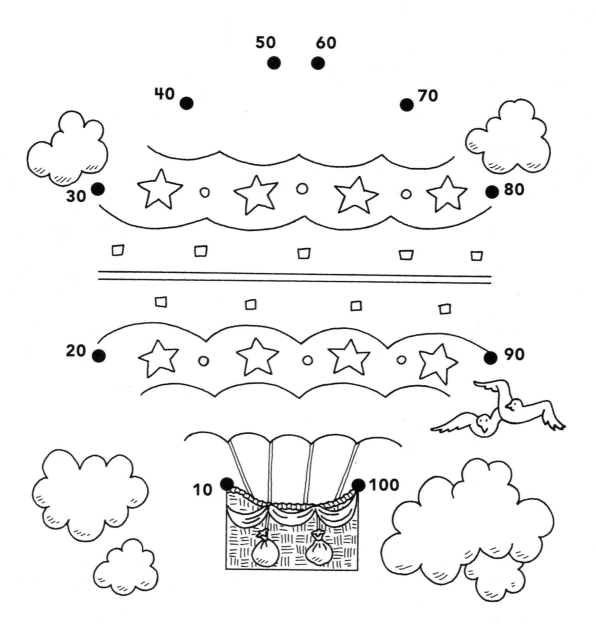

Name _____ Date _____

Teeth Totals

Look at Ali Gator's teeth.

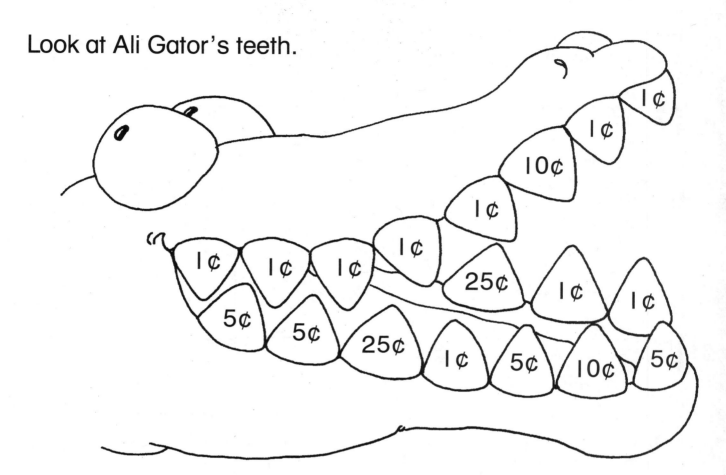

How many teeth?   How much money in all?

1. How many 1¢? ⬜   ⬜ cents

2. How many 5¢? ⬜   ⬜ cents

3. How many 10¢? ⬜   ⬜ cents

4. How many 25¢? ⬜   ⬜ cents

100 Math Practice Pages, Grade 1 © 2015 • Scholastic Teaching Resources

Number Juggle

Help each clown find the sum of the
two numbers. Write the number on the ball.

1 $17 + 2 = \bigcirc$

2 $15 + 4 = \bigcirc$

3 $30 + 7 = \bigcirc$

4 $22 + 7 = \bigcirc$

5 $20 + 20 = \bigcirc$

6 $11 + 22 = \bigcirc$

7 $10 + 35 = \bigcirc$

8 $42 + 3 = \bigcirc$

9 $40 + 10 = \bigcirc$

Name _____ Date _____

What did the big grape say to the little grape in December?

Add.

Solve the riddle using your answers.

13 +15	23 +11	10 + 6	42 + 7	10 +25	11 +16
___ S	___ H	___ O	___ A	___ T	___ N

44 + 4	34 +12	15 +11	50 + 0	32 +10	12 +11
___ B	___ J	___ Y	___ I	___ E	___ L

Solve the Riddle! Write the letter that goes with each number.

, ___ ___ ___ ___ ___ ___ ___ ___ ___ ___ ___ ___
 35 50 28   35 34 42   28 42 49 28 16 27

  ___ ___ ___ ___ ___ ___ ___ ___ ___ **!**
   35 16   48 42   46 42 23 23 26

Little Pig's Problem

Little Pig has a big problem! His homework got crushed in his book bag, and now he can't read it. To help Little Pig fix his homework, find each missing number. Then write the number in the box. Use the back of the page to show how you got your answers.

1
$$\begin{array}{r} 4\ \square \\ +\ \ \ 6 \\ \hline 4\ 9 \end{array}$$

2
$$\begin{array}{r} 3\ \square \\ +\ 1\ 3 \\ \hline 4\ 8 \end{array}$$

3
$$\begin{array}{r} 2\ 2 \\ +\ 1\ \square \\ \hline 3\ 6 \end{array}$$

4
$$\begin{array}{r} \square\ 4 \\ +\ 3\ \square \\ \hline 4\ 4 \end{array}$$

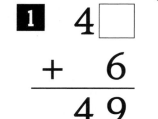

5
$$\begin{array}{r} \square\ 5 \\ +\ 1\ \square \\ \hline 3\ 5 \end{array}$$

6
$$\begin{array}{r} \square\ \square \\ +\ 3\ 0 \\ \hline 5\ 0 \end{array}$$

7
$$\begin{array}{r} 1\ \square \\ +\ \square\ 6 \\ \hline 4\ 9 \end{array}$$

8
$$\begin{array}{r} \square\ 5 \\ +\ 2\ \square \\ \hline 3\ 7 \end{array}$$

9
$$\begin{array}{r} \square\ 2 \\ +\ 2\ \square \\ \hline 4\ 4 \end{array}$$

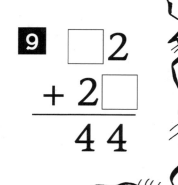

Name _____ Date _____

What dessert do kittens like best?

Regroup to add.
Solve the riddle using your answers.

```
   23        38        26        18        18        15
 + 9       + 8       + 9       +24       +29       +16
 _____    _____    _____    _____    _____    _____
   I         R         D         E         O         B
```

```
   27        28        19        38        25        19
 +17       +12       +18       + 7       +25       +29
 _____    _____    _____    _____    _____    _____
   M         A         C         S         F         N
```

Solve the Riddle!   Write the letter that goes with each number.

____ ____ ____ ____   ____ ____ ____ ____ ____
44   32   37   42   37   46   42   40   44

      ____ ____ ____ ____ ____
      37   47   48   42   45

100 Math Practice Pages, Grade 1 © 2015 • Scholastic Teaching Resources

Name _____   Date _____

Cross the River

Help the alligator cross the river.
Find the answer to each problem.

If the answer is	Color the space
Less than 20	Green
Greater than 20	Blue

Color Key

25 − 3	33 − 22	43 − 3	20 − 10
29 − 8	47 − 35	37 − 4	44 − 33
36 − 15	27 − 16	19 − 12	38 − 28
47 − 21	50 − 10	45 − 22	49 − 18

100 Math Practice Pages, Grade 1 © 2015 • Scholastic Teaching Resources

People and Pets

For each problem, find the difference between the age of the pet and its owner. Write an equation to show how you got your answer.

1

37 years   4 years

Sam is _____ years older than his dog.

2

28 years   2 years

Tina is _____ years older than her mouse.

3

10 years   50 years

Joe's turtle is _____ years older than Joe.

4

11 years   19 years

Ben's iguana is _____ years older than Ben.

5

4 years   15 years

Tara's cat is _____ years older than Tara.

6

47 years   3 years

Nick is _____ years older than his horse.

Name _____   Date _____

How did the band march in the parade?

Regroup to subtract.
Solve the riddle using your answers.

45	23	47	34	50	31
−28	−17	−29	−19	−29	−12
___	___	___	___	___	___
B	N	S	U	M	T

42	50	20	45	32	50
−19	−43	−11	−17	−16	−24
___	___	___	___	___	___
E	A	D	W	O	H

Solve the Riddle!   Write the letter that goes with each number.

___ ___ ___ ___   ___ ___ ___
19   15   17   7   19   28   16

100 Math Practice Pages, Grade 1 © 2015 • Scholastic Teaching Resources

Name _____ Date _____

Messy Math

Oops! A messy math student spilled jelly all over these math problems! Can you figure out which numbers are hidden?

1.

$$\begin{array}{r} 12 \\ +\quad \\ \hline 26 \end{array}$$

2.
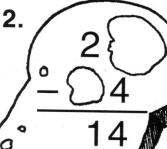

$$\begin{array}{r} 2 \\ -\ 4 \\ \hline 14 \end{array}$$

3.

$$\begin{array}{r} 2 \\ +\ 6 \\ \hline 99 \end{array}$$

4.
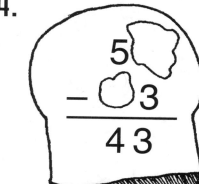

$$\begin{array}{r} 5 \\ -\ 3 \\ \hline 43 \end{array}$$

5.
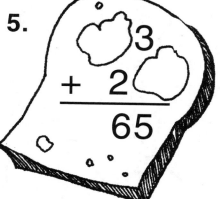

$$\begin{array}{r} 3 \\ +\ 2 \\ \hline 65 \end{array}$$

6.

$$\begin{array}{r} 39 \\ -\ 2 \\ \hline 18 \end{array}$$

7.

$$\begin{array}{r} 3 \\ -\ 22 \\ \hline 0 \end{array}$$

8.

$$\begin{array}{r} 8 \\ -\ 5 \\ \hline 24 \end{array}$$

100 Math Practice Pages, Grade 1 © 2015 • Scholastic Teaching Resources

Name _____   Date _____

Flying Butterflies

Solve each problem. Then find your answers in the key to see how to color the butterflies. Color the right wings to match the left wings.

1

$$\begin{array}{r} 18 \\ +\ 31 \\ \hline \end{array}$$

2

$$\begin{array}{r} 68 \\ -\ 43 \\ \hline \end{array}$$

3

$$\begin{array}{r} 54 \\ -\ 30 \\ \hline \end{array}$$

$$\begin{array}{r} 42 \\ -\ 16 \\ \hline \end{array}$$

4

$$\begin{array}{r} 39 \\ +\ 19 \\ \hline \end{array}$$

5

$$\begin{array}{r} 89 \\ -\ 31 \\ \hline \end{array}$$

$$\begin{array}{r} 24 \\ +\ 25 \\ \hline \end{array}$$

6

$$\begin{array}{r} 45 \\ -\ 21 \\ \hline \end{array}$$

$$\begin{array}{r} 22 \\ +\ 36 \\ \hline \end{array}$$

Name _____

Date _____

Acorn Hunt

Draw a picture to solve the problem.
Write the number sentence on the line.

Mindy picked up fourteen acorns.
Then she picked up five more acorns.
How many acorns does Mindy have?

_____ acorns

_____

1 . Color the 9th acorn.

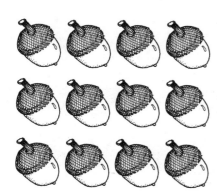

2. Color the 12th acorn.

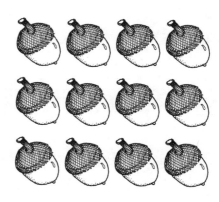

 100 Math Practice Pages, Grade 1 © 2015 • Scholastic Teaching Resources

Name _____ Date _____

Art Class

**Solve each word problem.
Show your work in the tank.**

1. Jalal draws
8 pictures of
animals. He draws
9 pictures of
boats. How many
pictures does
Jalal draw?

He draws

_____

pictures.

2. The art teacher
gets 32 new
paintbrushes and
45 new markers.
How many new
art items is this
in all?

_____ new

art items

Fruit Fun

Put on your thinking cap to solve each word problem.

Draw a picture to help solve the problem.

1. Ciera planted three strawberry bushes. Then she planted six blueberry bushes.

   How many bushes did Ciera plant in all? _____

2. Dennis planted twelve apple trees and twelve cherry trees.

   How many trees did Dennis plant in all? _____

3. Syd baked one apple pie, three cherry pies, and four blueberry pies.

   How many pies did Syd bake in all? _____

Name _____ Date _____

Piggy Bank

Draw a picture to solve the word problem.
Write the number sentence on the line.

Jenny had 10¢ in her piggy bank.
Her grandmother gave her 5 pennies.

How much money does Jenny have now? _____

_____

Quick
Review

Compare the value of the coins. Write >, <, or = on each line.

1.

2. _____

3.

Name _____ Date _____

Dollars and Cents

Complete each problem.

Libby has a dime. Then she finds 2 pennies. Now how much money does Libby have?

_____ cents

After school, Hakim buys an apple for 20¢. He also buys string cheese for 75¢. How much does he spend on his snack?

He spends _____ ¢.

Zaria buys an ice pop for one dollar. She buys a finger puppet for three dollars. How much money does she spend?

_____ dollars

Nathan buys 2 toy cars. They cost $2 each. How much does he spend on toy cars?

$ _____

Name _____   Date _____

Stamp Subtraction

Draw a picture to solve the problem.
Write the number sentence on the line.

Caroline had nineteen stamps.
She used thirteen stamps.

How many stamps does Caroline have left?   _____ stamps

_____

 **Quick Review** _____

Count backwards.

1. _____, 11, _____, 9   2. _____, 16, 15, _____

3. _____, 19, _____, 17   4. _____, 12, _____, 10

Name _____   Date _____

School Days

**Solve each word problem.
Show your work in the tank.**

1. Geena has 8 books.
She did not read 2
of them. How many
books did she read?

She read _____
books.

2. Edgar has 8 crayons.
He gives some to
Ana. Then Edgar
has 5 crayons. How
many did Ana get?

Ana got _____
crayons.

Name _____   Date _____

Baking Fun

Put on your thinking cap to solve each word problem.

Draw a picture to help you solve the problem.

1. George made twelve cookies.
   Then he ate four cookies.

   How many cookies
   does George have left? _____

2. Serena poured eight cups of milk.
   She gave three cups to her friends.

   How many cups of milk
   does Serena have left? _____

3. Thomas made twenty-four muffins.
   He brought twenty-one to share with
   his class.

   How many muffins does
   Thomas still have at home? _____

Name _____ Date _____

Party Time

Solve each word problem. Show your work in the tank.

1. Margo has 10 nickels.
   She spends 3 of
   them on balloons.
   How many nickels
   does Margo
   still have?

   Margo has

   _____ nickels.

   It is the same as

   _____ cents.

2. Van has 30¢.
   He buys a mini
   glow stick for 15¢.
   How much money
   does he still have?

   Van still has

   _____ ¢.

100 Math Practice Pages, Grade 1 © 2015 • Scholastic Teaching Resources

Name _____ Date _____

Weekend Math

Complete each problem.

There are 28 children at the pizza parlor. There are 15 boys. How many children are girls? There are

_____ girls.

On the hike, Carly saw 11 birds. Rob saw 8 birds. Who saw fewer?

_____

How many fewer?

_____

Ondie buys ribbons. She gets a red one for 15¢. She gets a purple one for 10¢. She gets a silver one for 25¢. How much does Ondie spend in all?

_____ ¢

The coach serves fruit snacks. She gives bananas to 14 kids. She gives oranges to 9 kids. How many more kids snack on bananas than on oranges?

_____

Name _____ Date _____

Growing Flowers

Draw a picture to show to solve the problem.
Write the number sentence on the line.

Ben planted 13 flowers in a flower pot. He planted
15 flowers in another flower pot. He picked one flower
from each pot to give to his grandmother.

How many flowers does Ben have left?   _____ flowers

_____

How many legs?

1. _____ legs

2. _____ legs

Name _____ Date _____

Playtime

Solve each word problem.
Show your work in the tank.

1. Eli has 22 marbles. He keeps 12 of them. He gives the rest to his 2 sisters. Each gets the same number.

   How many marbles does each sister get?

   _____ marbles each.

2. Sixty-five children go ice skating. Twelve of them go inside to rest. Five of them return to the rink after a few minutes.

   How many children are now skating?

   _____

Snack Time

Put on your thinking cap to solve
each word problem.

Draw a picture to help you solve the problem.

1. Amy had 6 carrot sticks. She ate
   2 carrot sticks. Then her mother
   gave her 4 more carrot sticks.

   How many carrot sticks
   does Amy have left? _____

2. Danny had 15 blueberries.
   His sister gave him 5 more berries.
   Then he ate 10 in all.

   How many blueberries
   does Danny still have? _____

3. I have a bag of popcorn. I share
   the popcorn with two friends.

   My friends each share some of the
   popcorn with two friends.
   How many people have popcorn? _____

Animal Math

Complete each problem.

Buster buried 18 bones last week. Yesterday, he buried 3 more. He dug up 6 bones today. How many bones are still buried?

_____ bones

Squirrel had 13 acorns in her nest. She moved 7 more acorns to her nest. Then 4 acorns fell to the ground. How many acorns are left in Squirrel's nest?

_____ acorns

Ten ants crawled up a fence. Six more ants joined them. Thirteen ants crawled back down the fence. How many ants are still on the fence?

_____ ants

Seven snakes hid under a bush. Eight more snakes joined them. One snake slithered away. How many snakes are still under the bush?

_____ snakes

Name _____ Date _____

Longest and Shortest

Look at each set of pictures below.
Then follow the directions.

1

Circle the longest one.

2

Circle the shortest one.

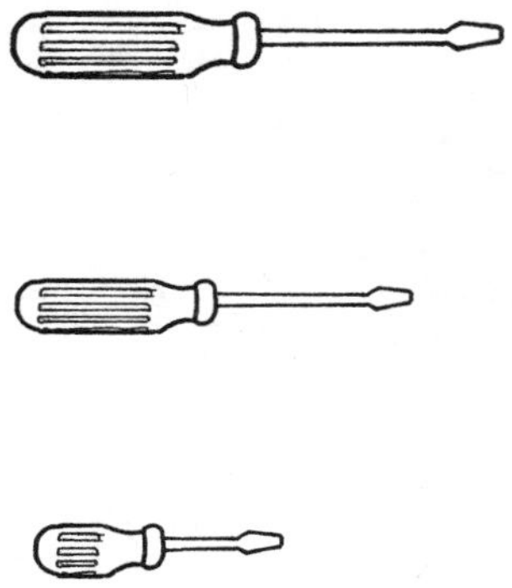

3

Circle the shortest one.

4

Circle the longest one.

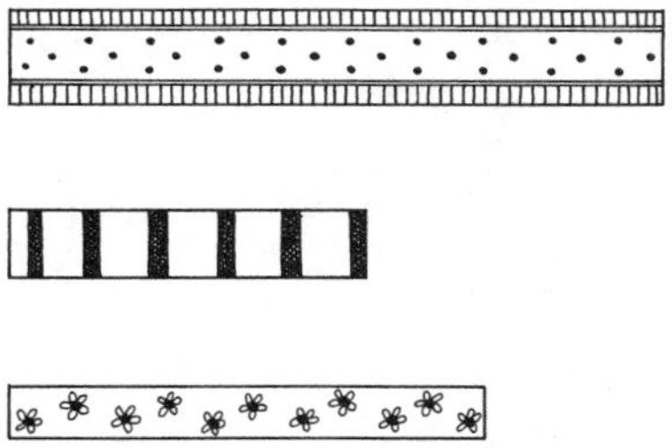

100 Math Practice Pages, Grade 1 © 2015 • Scholastic Teaching Resources

Name _____ Date _____

In Real Life . . .

Put on your thinking cap and circle each answer.

1. In real life, which one is the longest?

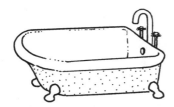  

2. In real life, which one is the shortest?

Name _____ Date _____

How Long Is It?

How many erasers long is each item? Write the answer.

1.

_____ erasers

2.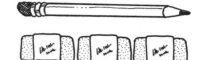

_____ erasers

3.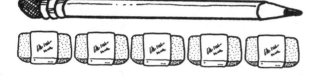

_____ erasers

4.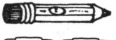

_____ erasers

 Quick Review

1. Circle the longest one.

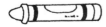

2. Circle the shortest one.

Name _____ Date _____

Tool Time

How many leaves long is each item?
Write the answer.

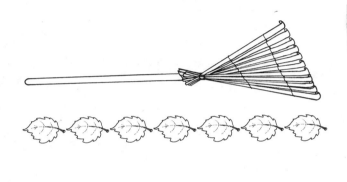

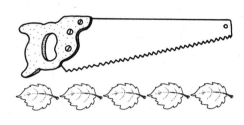

_____ leaves

_____ leaves

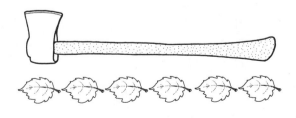

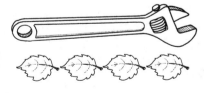

_____ leaves

_____ leaves

100 Math Practice Pages, Grade 1 © 2015 • Scholastic Teaching Resources

Name _____ Date _____

Length Hunt

Do a length hunt. Use your hand as a "ruler."
Find 3 things for each part of the chart. List them.

Shorter than my hand	About the Same as my hand	Longer than my hand

Look at the boxes. Then draw each line. Start at ● .

Draw a line about 7 boxes long.

  ●

Draw a line about 2 boxes long.

  ●

Draw a line longer than 10 boxes.

  ●

Order the lines from 1 (longest) to 3 (shortest).
Write the numbers in the circles.

100 Math Practice Pages, Grade 1 © 2015 • Scholastic Teaching Resources

Name _____ Date _____

Silly Snakes

How many inches long is each item? Write the answer.

1.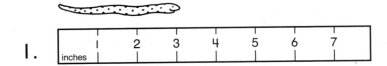

_____ inches

2.

_____ inches

3.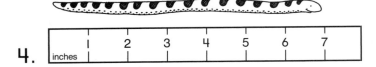

_____ inches

4.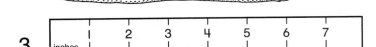

_____ inches

 Quick Review

1. How much longer is rope A than rope B?

A 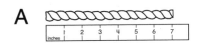   B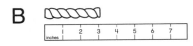

_____ inches

2. How much shorter is pencil B than pencil A?

A 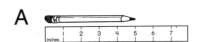   B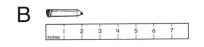

_____ inches

Name _____ Date _____

Pretty Eggs

Read the word in each egg.

Which tool would you use to measure it?

If the answer is	Color the egg
ruler	Yellow
measuring tape	Green

Color Key

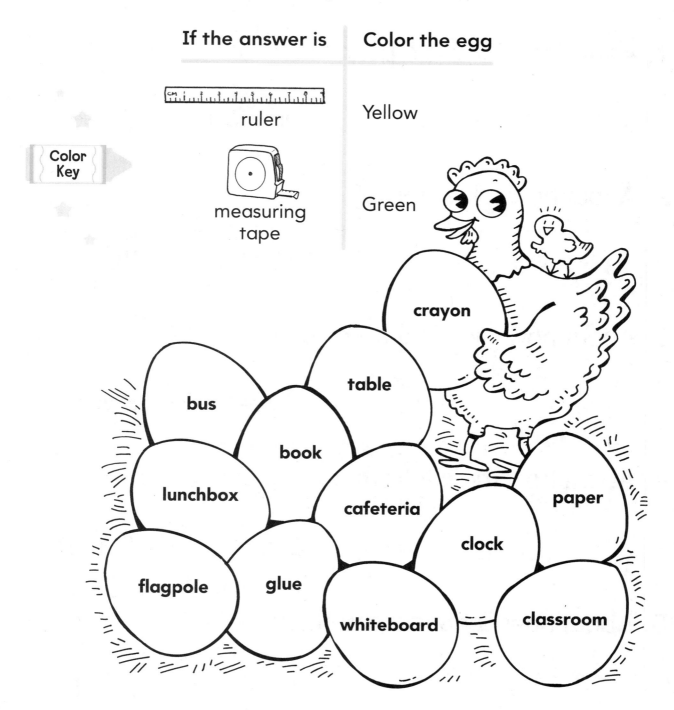

crayon

bus

table

book

lunchbox

cafeteria

paper

flagpole

glue

clock

whiteboard

classroom

Name _____ Date _____

What Is Your Estimate?

Put on your thinking cap and
circle the best estimate.

1. About how long is a pencil?

    7 inches   7 feet

2. About how tall is a tree?

    40 inches   40 feet

3. About how wide is a doorway?

    3 feet   3 yards

4. About how far is it from your house to the store?

    2 yards   2 miles

5. About how deep is a swimming pool?

    10 feet   10 miles

Name _____ Date _____

What Time Is It?

Look at the clocks below.
Write the time each clock shows.

1  ____ : ____	**2**  ____ : ____
3  ____ : ____	**4**  ____ : ____
5  ____ : ____	**6**  ____ : ____
7  ____ : ____	**8**  ____ : ____

Name _____ Date _____

Ready for Bed

If the time on the clock matches			Color the space
8:00	or	11:00	Blue
8:30	or	11:30	Red
6:00	or	9:00	Yellow
3:00	or	4:30	Green

Color Key

Name _____ Date _____

Tick-Tock Clocks

Draw hands to show each time.

2:00

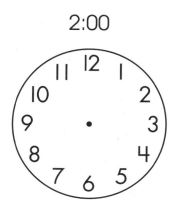

6:00

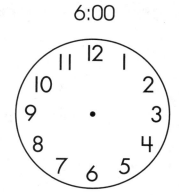

11:00

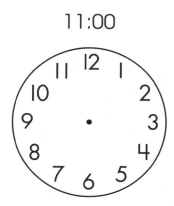

10:30

9:00

5:30

9:00

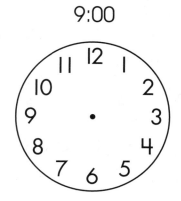

100 Math Practice Pages, Grade 1 © 2015 • Scholastic Teaching Resources

How Much Time?

Look at the first clock.
Then look at the second clock.
How much time has passed?

_____ hours

_____ hours

_____ hours

_____ hours

Name _____ Date _____

When Do I . . . ?

Match the time of day to an activity.

7:30 P.M.

7:00 A.M.

11:00 A.M.

10:00 P.M.

4:00 P.M.

Name _____ Date _____

Time for a Mix-Up

Unscramble the letters! Write the correct time words on the lines. Use the Word Bank to help.

1. decons _____

2. nutime _____

3. ohru _____

4. yad _____

5. kewe _____

6. notmh _____

7. arey _____

8. occlk _____

10. hdna _____

Word Bank	
clock	day
hand	hour
minute	month
second	watch
week	year

Ways to Tell Time

Match each picture to the name of the time-keeping device.

hour glass

wrist watch

kitchen timer

cuckoo clock

alarm clock

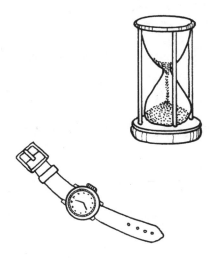

grandfather clock

Name _____ Date _____

How Long Does It Take?

Put on your thinking cap and circle the best estimate.

About how long does it take . . .

1. to brush your teeth?

    2 seconds   2 minutes   2 hours

2. to laugh at a joke?

    3 seconds   3 minutes   3 hours

3. to set the table for dinner?

    5 seconds   5 minutes   5 hours

4. to play catch?

    15 seconds   15 minutes   15 hours

5. to do your homework?

    1 second   1 minute   1 hour

100 Math Practice Pages, Grade 1 © 2015 • Scholastic Teaching Resources

Name _____   Date _____

It's Time!

Complete each problem.

Fill in the missing numbers on the clock.

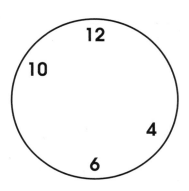

Circle your answer. When do you get to school?

morning   afternoon   night

When do you eat dinner?

morning   afternoon   night

What is another way to say 12:00 A.M.?

_____

What is another way to say 12:00 P.M.?

_____

What time is it now? Be sure to include A.M. or P.M.

_____ : _____ _____

What time will it be in 2 hours?

_____ : _____ _____

Name _____ Date _____

Data Hunt

Look around you. How many of each
item do you see?

1 How many of these things are you wearing?

buttons _____   zippers _____

snaps _____   ties _____

2 Look around the room and count how many:

windows _____   doors _____

plants _____   clocks _____

3 Write the first name of 5 people you know.

_____   _____

_____   _____

_____

How many vowels are in their names?

a _____   e _____   i _____

o _____   u _____

Name _____ Date _____

Winter Wear

Use the graph to answer the questions.

hat	🎩	🎩	🎩	🎩	🎩	🎩	🎩	🎩	
mitten	🧤	🧤	🧤	🧤	🧤	🧤			
scarf	🧣	🧣	🧣	🧣	🧣	🧣	🧣	🧣	🧣
	1	2	3	4	5	6	7	8	9

1. How many of each item?

   hats: _____   mittens: _____   scarves: _____

2. How many mittens and scarves in all? _____

3. How many hats and scarves in all? _____

4. How many more scarves than mittens? _____

Quick Review _____

Count the shirts.

1. _____   2. _____   3. _____

Name _____ Date _____

See Our Seashells!

Use the graph to answer the questions.

Seashells We Found

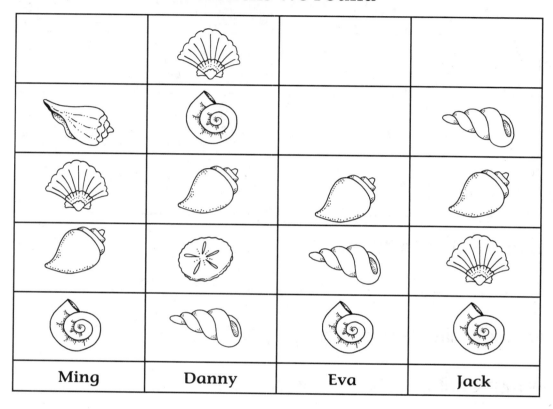

| Ming | Danny | Eva | Jack |

1. How many children found shells? _____

2. How many shells did the children find in all? _____

3. Who found the fewest shells? _____

4. Two children found 4 shells each. Write their names.

_____ and _____

5. Who found the most shells? _____

Graph Time

First study the graph and key.
Then use them to answer the questions.

Best Things to Collect

Leaves	☺ ☺ ☺
Rocks	☺ ☺ ☺ ☺ ☺ ☺
Shells	☺ ☺ ☺ ☺ ☺ ☺ ☺ ☺ ☺
Key: ☺ = 1 vote	

How many votes does ☺ represent?

_____

Add your vote to the graph.

How many people voted for rocks?

_____

How many people voted for leaves?

_____

Which is the favorite thing to collect?

_____

How many people picked it?

_____

What's the Weather?

Use the calendar to answer the questions.

Weather in May

Sunday	Monday	Tuesday	Wednesday	Thursday	Friday	Saturday
1	2	3	4	5	6	7

1. How many days in a week? _____

2. How many days had ? _____

3. How many days had ? _____

4. What was the weather on Thursday? _____

5. Which were bad days for being outdoors? _____

_____

Counting Critters

Use the graph to answer the questions.

	1	2	3	4	5	6	7	8	9
rabbit	🐰	🐰	🐰						
mouse	🐭	🐭	🐭	🐭	🐭	🐭			
skunk	🦨	🦨	🦨	🦨					
	1	2	3	4	5	6	7	8	9

1. How many of each animal?

   rabbits: _____   mice: _____   skunks: _____

2. How many more mice than rabbits? _____

3. How many more skunks than rabbits? _____

4. How many mice and skunks? _____

Write the number.

1. _____   2. _____   3. _____

Name _____ Date _____

We're Thirsty!

Mrs. Greene took her class to lunch. She saw that 6 kids drank juice, 9 drank milk, and 7 kids drank water.

Show this data in a graph.
Make bars with letters.
Count from the bottom up.

- Write a **J** for each juice.

- Write an **M** for each milk.

- Write a **W** for each water.

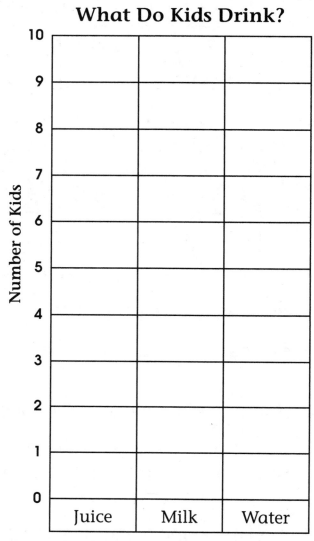

What Do Kids Drink?

Number of Kids

| | Juice | Milk | Water |

Kind of Drink

1. How many kids were at lunch? _____

2. Which drink did most kids choose? _____

3. How many kids drank water or juice? _____

Name _____ Date _____

Perfect Pets

Some children shared their idea of a perfect pet.
Complete the graph. Color a box for each item.

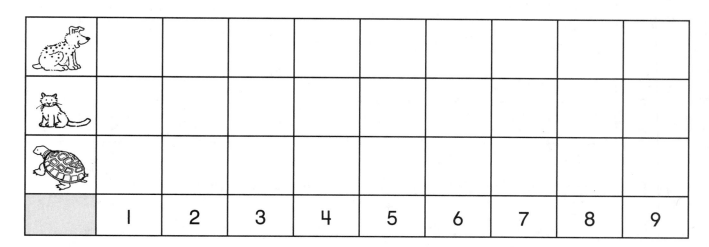

1. How many children voted? _____

2. Circle the animal that most of the children chose.

3. How many more children chose turtles than dogs?

_____

Write the number sentence. _____

100 Math Practice Pages, Grade 1 © 2015 • Scholastic Teaching Resources

Name _____ Date _____

Around the Farm

Complete the graph. Color a box for each animal.

	1	2	3	4	5	6	7	8	9
🐷									
🐄									
🐔									

1. There are five of which animal? Circle the answer.

2. How many more cows than pigs? _____

   Write the number sentence. _____

3. How many more cows than hens? _____

   Write the number sentence. _____

Name _____ Date _____

Animal Tally

Complete the graph.
Color a box for each animal.

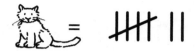 = |||| ||| = |||| ||

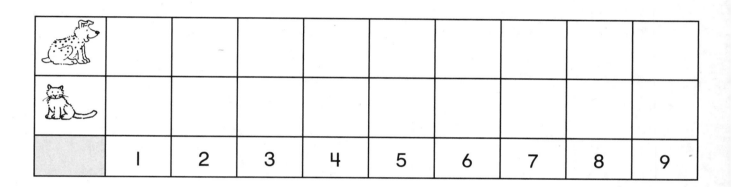

	1	2	3	4	5	6	7	8	9

1. How many dogs? _____

2. How many cats? _____

3. How many dogs and cats? _____

   Write the number sentence. _____

4. How many more dogs than cats? _____

   Write the number sentence. _____

5. Write tally marks to show how many dogs and cats in all.

   _____

100 Math Practice Pages, Grade 1 © 2015 • Scholastic Teaching Resources

Name _____   Date _____

Word Search

Circle the geometry words from the word box. You can find the words going across or down. One has been done for you.

Word Box			
circle	square	rectangle	triangle
sphere	cube	cylinder	cone
pyramid	pentagon	hexagon	

```
H  D  B  H  E  X  A  G  O  N
P  M  D  F  X  H  P  P  U  R
E  Y  A  I  L  X  C  Y  C  E
N  C  I  R  C  L  E  R  Y  C
T  C  W  H  A  N  C  A  L  T
A  C  O  N  E  X  U  M  I  A
G  Q  Z  M  V  U  B  I  N  N
O  S  P  H  E  R  E  D  D  G
N  K  E  S  Q  U  A  R  E  L
T  R  I  A  N  G  L  E  R  E
```

Name _____ Date _____

Space City

Find each shape	Color that shape
◯	Red
▢	Blue
△	Green
▯	Yellow

Color Key

100 Math Practice Pages, Grade 1 © 2015 • Scholastic Teaching Resources

Name _____ Date _____

Find the Shape

Follow the directions below.

Color the squares.

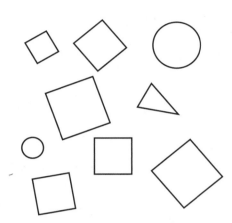

How many stars? _____

How many pentagons? _____

Color the rectangles.

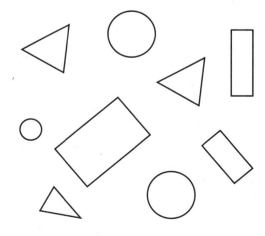

100 Math Practice Pages, Grade 1 © 2015 • Scholastic Teaching Resources

Name _____ Date _____

Castle Count

Find	Trace each of those shapes
7 rectangles	Blue
8 triangles	Red
9 circles	Orange
10 squares	Yellow

Color Key

100 Math Practice Pages, Grade 1 © 2015 • Scholastic Teaching Resources

Name _____ Date _____

Shop for Shapes

Write how much each
shape combination costs.

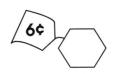 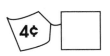

1

_____

2

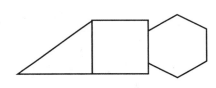

_____

3

_____

4

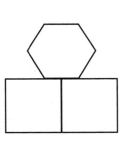

_____

5

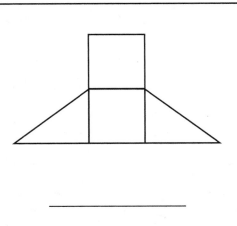

_____

6

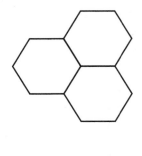

_____

100 Math Practice Pages, Grade 1 © 2015 • Scholastic Teaching Resources

Name _____   Date _____

Shape Trace

Trace the shapes. Then use the key to color
in the shapes.

Key	
Shape	**Color**
⬭	orange
△	green
◯	yellow
▢	brown
▭	blue
⬡	red

100 Math Practice Pages, Grade 1 © 2015 • Scholastic Teaching Resources

Name _____ Date _____

Shaping Up

Make the shapes.

100 Math Practice Pages, Grade 1 © 2015 • Scholastic Teaching Resources

Name _____ Date _____

Train Game

Draw a train. Use these shapes:

- 2 rectangles • 2 squares • 2 triangles • 4 circles

Quick Review

1. Color the square.

2. Color the circle.

3. Color the rectangle.

100 Math Practice Pages, Grade 1 © 2015 • Scholastic Teaching Resources

Name _____ Date _____

Make More Shapes

Follow the directions below.

Draw a line to make
two squares.

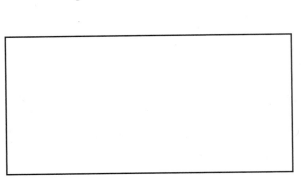

Draw a line to make
two triangles.

Draw a line to make
two triangles.

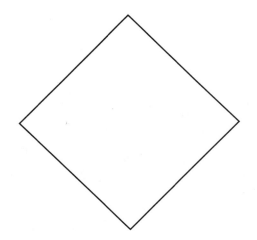

Draw a line to make two
rectangles.

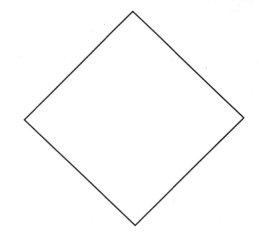

Name _____ Date _____

Corners and Sides

How many corners are in each shape?

1. [square] _____ corners

2. 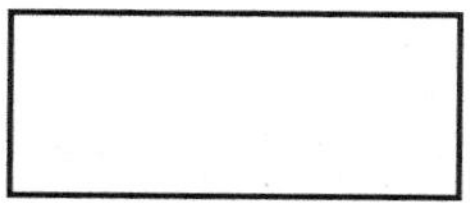 [rectangle] _____ corners

3. 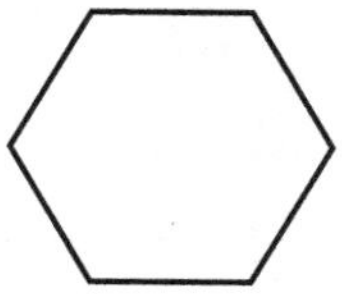 [hexagon] _____ corners

4. 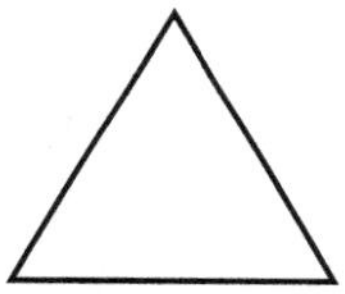 [triangle] _____ corners

5. 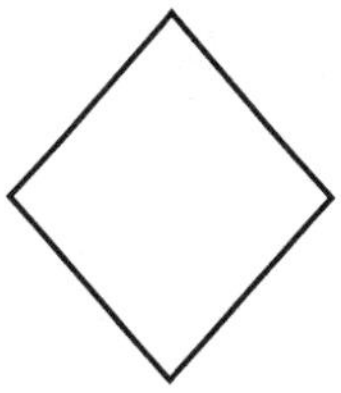 [diamond] _____ corners

6. 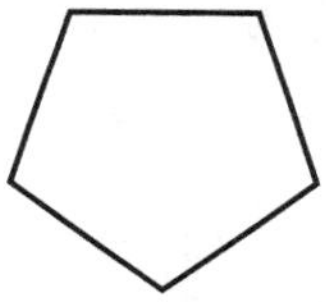 [pentagon] _____ corners

How many sides are in each shape?

7. square _____

8. triangle _____

9. rectangle _____

10. pentagon _____

Name _____ Date _____

Complete the Shape

Draw the other half of each shape. Example:

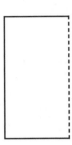 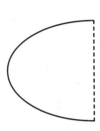 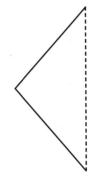

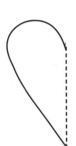 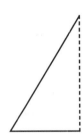

Match each item to its shape.

It's a Draw

Complete each problem.

Draw a large square and
a small square.

Draw two circles. Make
them the same size.

Show two different ways
to cut a square in half.

Follow these directions
on the back of this paper.

- Draw a rectangle.

- Draw 3 circles inside
  the rectangle.

- Draw a triangle inside
  each circle.

Name _____ Date _____

Just Geometry

Put on your thinking cap to solve these problems!

1. How many sides in each shape?

          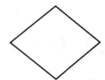

_____ sides   _____ sides   _____ sides

2. Circle the name of each shape.

cone   cube   sphere   cylinder   cube   sphere

3. Find each shape sum.
   Use the numbers in
   the shapes.

③ △4 ⑤

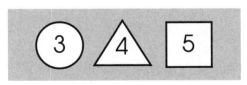 = _____

Practice Page 1:

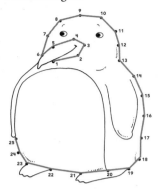

Practice Page 2:

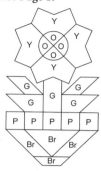

Practice Page 3:

in the dark

A-31, E-28, H-34, N-36, T-43, S-42, D-30, F-29, I-40, K-38, R-41, W-49

Practice Page 4:

2, 4, 5, 3, 6; 3, 7, 4, 10, 6

Practice Page 5:

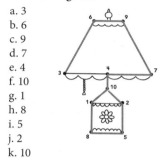

Practice Page 6:

ferry tales

A-55, C-56, G-53, I-57, R-71, T-68, B-59, F-51, E-60, L-69, S-74, Y-72

Practice Page 7:

75, 81, 84, 79, 87, 91, 96, 100

Practice Page 8:

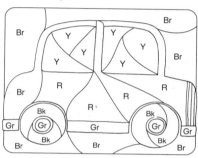

Practice Page 9:

Practice Page 10:

Check students' work; fifth

Practice Page 11:

1. 7 + 5 = 12; 12
2. 9 + 6 = 15; 15
3. 7 + 6 = 13; 13
4. 6 + 8 = 14; 14
5. 9 + 8 = 17; 17
6. 4 + 7 = 11; 11

Practice Page 12:

1. 5 − 2 = 3
2. 12 − 5 = 7
3. 12 − 6 = 6

Practice Page 13:

1. 6
2. 8
3. 7
4. 3
5. 3
6. 1

Practice Page 14:

Answers will vary.

Practice Page 15:

chocolate chirp

A-8, C-6, H-9, S-11, R-4, O-5, L-3, E-10, P-1, T-2, I-7, N-12

Practice Page 16:

1. 10 − 3 = 7; 7
2. 10 − 5 = 5; 5
3. 10 − 8 = 2; 2
4. 10 − 2 = 8; 8
5. 10 − 4 = 6; 6
6. 10 − 6 = 4; 4
7. 10 − 7 = 3; 3
8. 10 − 9 = 1; 1
9. 10 − 1 = 9; 9

Practice Page 17:

a. 3
b. 6
c. 9
d. 7
e. 4
f. 10
g. 1
h. 8
i. 5
j. 2
k. 10

Practice Page 18:

It waves.

$$5 + ③ + ⑦ = \frac{15}{I}$$

$$③ + ⑦ + 4 = \frac{14}{W}$$

$$3 + ⑥ + ④ = \frac{13}{S}$$

$$⑤ + 1 + ⑤ = \frac{11}{R}$$

$$2 + 7 + ⑧ = \frac{17}{E}$$

$$⑥ + ④ + 9 = \frac{19}{V}$$

$$⑥ + 2 + ④ = \frac{12}{N}$$

$$⑧ + ② + 10 = \frac{20}{A}$$

$$⑤ + 8 + ⑤ = \frac{18}{T}$$

Practice Page 19:

Practice Page 20:
1. 2; 1 + 1 = 2
2. 6; 3 + 3 = 6
3. 8; 4 + 4 = 8
4. 10; 5 + 5 = 10
5. 18; 9 + 9 = 18
6. 14; 7 + 7 = 14
7. 22; 11 + 11 = 21
8. 24; 12 + 12 = 24

Practice Page 21:
He was too unhoppy.
A-16, H-22, E-18, N-23, O-25, T-14, Y-11, S-19, W-6, U-20, P-24, R-9

Practice Page 22:
Students should circle five sets of ten bees.
5 tens, 1 ones
51
Quick Review

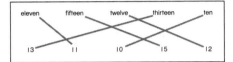

Practice Page 23:

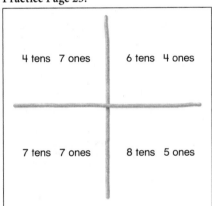

4 tens   7 ones   6 tens   4 ones

7 tens   7 ones   8 tens   5 ones

Practice Page 24:
14, 15, 16, 17, 18, 19

Practice Page 25:
am-fib-ians
F-30, S-56, E-35, R-28, N-91, I-63, M-66, B-40, A-87, P-72

Practice Page 26:

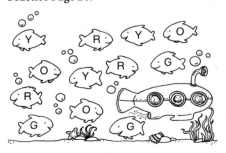

Practice Page 27:
How many hours in a day?
24
Quick Review
1. 33
2. 55

Practice Page 28:
Numbers < 25—0, 6, 12, 15, 24;
Numbers 26 to 70—28, 33, 49, 54, 67;
Numbers > 70—71, 77, 82, 99, 100

Practice Page 29:

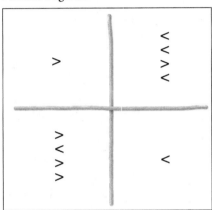

Practice Page 30:
1. <
2. >
3. <
4. >
5. >
6. <
Quick Review
1. Students should color the 3rd grape.
2. Students should color the 5th grape.

Practice Page 31:

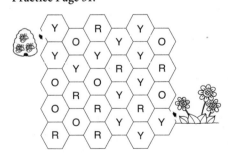

Practice Page 32:

26, 28 33, 35 60, 63	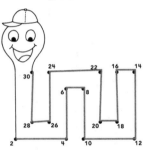
< > >	14, 24 12, 12

Practice Page 33:

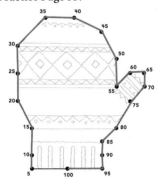

Practice Page 34:
buttered pup-corn
B-34, D-40, P-24, N-44, U-22, R-28, O-16, A-32, T-18, E-6, C-20, S-10

Practice Page 35:

Practice Page 36:

Practice Page 37:
1. 10, 10
2. 4, 20
3. 2, 20
4. 2, 50

Practice Page 38:
1. 19
2. 19
3. 37
4. 29
5. 40
6. 33
7. 45
8. 45
9. 50

Practice Page 39:
'Tis the season to be jelly!
S-28, H-34, O-16, A-49, T-35, N-27, B-48, J-46, Y-26, I-50, E-42, L-23

Practice Page 40:

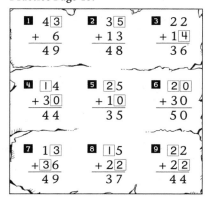

Practice Page 41:
mice cream cones
I-32, R-46, D-35, E-42, O-47, B-31, M-44, A-40, C-37, S-45, F-50, N-48

Practice Page 42:

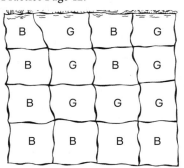

Practice Page 43:
1. 33 years $\begin{array}{r} 37 \\ -\ 4 \\ \hline 33 \end{array}$ **2.** 26 years $\begin{array}{r} 28 \\ -\ 2 \\ \hline 26 \end{array}$

3. 40 years $\begin{array}{r} 50 \\ -\ 10 \\ \hline 40 \end{array}$ **4.** 8 years $\begin{array}{r} 19 \\ -\ 11 \\ \hline 8 \end{array}$

5. 11 years $\begin{array}{r} 15 \\ -\ 4 \\ \hline 11 \end{array}$ **6.** 44 years $\begin{array}{r} 47 \\ -\ 3 \\ \hline 44 \end{array}$

Practice Page 44:
tuba two
B-17, N-6, S-18, U-15, M-21, T-19, E-23, A-7, D-9, W-28, O-16, H-26

Practice Page 45:
1. 12 + 14 = 26
2. 28 – 14 = 14
3. 32 + 67 = 99
4. 56 – 13 = 43
5. 43 + 22 = 65
6. 39 – 21 = 18
7. 32 – 22 = 10
8. 89 – 65 = 24

Practice Page 46:
1. 49; Y
2. 25; B
3. 24, 26; W, O
4. 58; P
5. 58, 49; P, Y
6. 24, 58; W, P

Practice Page 47:
Students should draw a set of 14 acorns and a set of 5 acorns.
19 acorns
14 + 5 = 19
Quick Review
1. Students should color the 9th acorn.
2. Students should color the 12th acorn.

Practice Page 48:
1. 17
2. 77

Practice Page 49:
1. 9 bushes
2. 24 trees
3. 8 pies

Practice Page 50:
Students should draw any combination of coins that equals 10¢, then draw 5 pennies.
15¢
10 + 5 = 15
Quick Review
1. <
2. =
3. <

Practice Page 51:

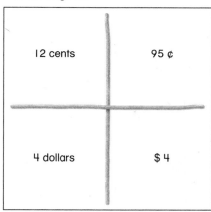

Practice Page 52:
Students should draw 19 stamps, then cross out 13.
6 stamps
19 – 13 = 6
Quick Review
1. 12, 10
2. 17, 14
3. 20, 18
4. 13, 11

Practice Page 53:
1. 6 **2.** 3

Practice Page 54:
1. 8 cookies
2. 5 cups
3. 3 muffins

Practice Page 55:
1. 7, 35 **2.** 15

Practice Page 56:

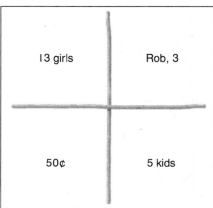

Practice Page 57:
Students should draw 13 flowers plus 15 flowers, then cross out 2.
26 flowers
13 + 15 – 2 = 26
Quick Review
1. 12
2. 24

Practice Page 58:
1. 5
2. 58

Practice Page 59:
1. 8 carrot sticks
2. 10 blueberries
3. 7 people

Practice Page 60:

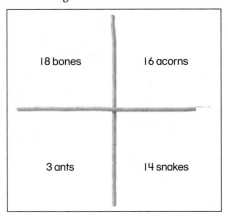

18 bones	16 acorns
3 ants	14 snakes

Practice Page 61:
1. Students should circle the bottom nail.
2. Students should circle the bottom screwdriver.
3. Students should circle the middle snake.
4. Students should circle the top ribbon.

Practice Page 62:
1. Students should circle the bus
2. Students should circle the rabbit.

Practice Page 63:
1. 4
2. 3
3. 5
4. 2
Quick Review
1. Students should circle the paintbrush.
2. Students should circle the glue stick.

Practice Page 64:

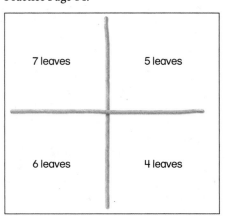

7 leaves	5 leaves
6 leaves	4 leaves

Practice Page 65:
Objects students find will vary; check for reasonableness.
Check students' lines.
2, 3, 1

Practice Page 66:
1. 3
2. 4
3. 6
4. 7
Quick Review
1. 4
2. 3

Practice Page 67:

Practice Page 68:
1. 7 inches
2. 40 feet
3. 3 feet
4. 2 miles
5. 10 feet

Practice Page 69:
1. 12:30 **2.** 4:30 **3.** 8:30 **4.** 2:30 **5.** 4:00 **6.** 7:00
7. 10:00 **8.** 1:00

Practice Page 70:

Practice Page 71:
Check students' clock-face drawings.

Practice Page 72:

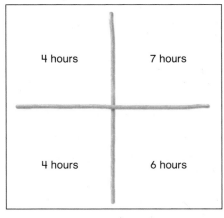

4 hours	7 hours
4 hours	6 hours

Practice Page 73:

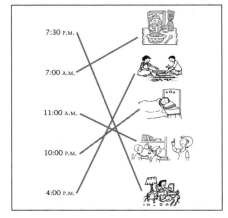

Practice Page 74:
1. second
2. minute
3. hour
4. day
5. week
6. month
7. year
8. clock
9. watch
10. hand

Practice Page 75:

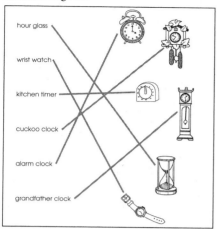

Practice Page 76:
1. 2 minutes
2. 3 seconds
3. 5 minutes
4. 15 minutes
5. 1 hour

Practice Page 77:

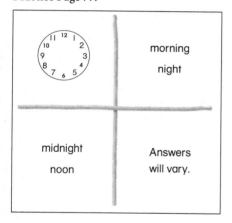

Practice Page 78:
1. Answers will vary; check for reasonableness.
2. Answers will vary; check for reasonableness.
3. Answers will vary; check students' work.

Practice Page 79:
1. 8, 6, 9
2. 15
3. 17
4. 3
Quick Review
1. 10
2. 6
3. 9

Practice Page 80:
1. 4 2. 16 3. Eva 4. Ming, Jack 5. Danny

Practice Page 81:

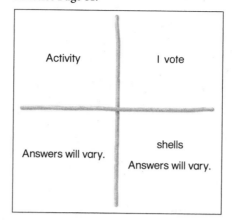

Practice Page 82:
1. 7
2. 3
3. 2
4. sunny
5. Tuesday and Friday

Practice Page 83:
1. 3, 6, 4
2. 3
3. 1
4. 10
Quick Review
1. 10
2. 13
3. 7

Practice Page 84:

	M	
	M	
	M	W
J	M	W
J	M	W
J	M	W
J	M	W
J	M	W
J	M	W
Juice	Milk	Water

1. 22 2. milk 3. 13

Practice Page 85:
Students should color 3 boxes for the dog, 5 boxes for the cat, and 4 boxes for the turtle.
1. 12
2. Students should circle the cat.
3. 1; 4 − 3 = 1

Practice Page 86:
Students should color 3 boxes for the pig, 8 boxes for the cow, and 5 boxes for the hen.
1. Students should circle the hen.
2. 5; 8 − 3 = 5
3. 3; 8 − 5 = 3

Practice Page 87:
Students should color 8 boxes for the dog and 7 boxes for the cat.
1. 8
2. 7
3. 15; 8 + 7 = 15
4. 1; 8 − 7 = 1
5. IIII IIII IIII

Practice Page 88:

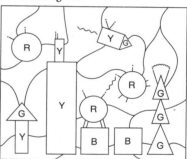

Practice Page 89:

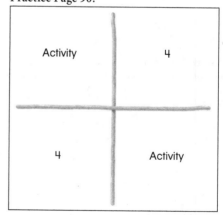

Practice Page 90:

Activity   4

4   Activity

Practice Page 91:
Students should trace the correct number of each shape with the appropriate color.

Practice Page 92:
1. 12¢ 2. 10¢ 3. 14¢ 4. 13¢ 5. 14¢ 6. 18¢

Practice Page 93:
Check students' coloring.

Practice Page 94:
Check students' shapes.

Practice Page 95:
Students should use the shapes to draw a train.
Quick Review
1. Students should color the square.
2. Students should color the circle.
3. Students should color the rectangle.

Practice Page 96:

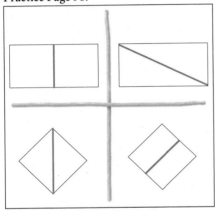

Practice Page 97:
1. 4
2. 4
3. 6
4. 3
5. 4
6. 5
7. 4
8. 3
9. 4
10. 5

Practice Page 98:
Students should draw the other half of each shape.
Quick Review

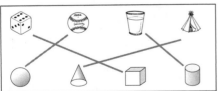

Practice Page 99:

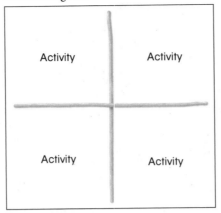

Practice Page 100:
1. 0, 3, 4
2. Students should circle *cone, cylinder, cube*.
3. 8, 13